# History or Un-history, The Crucial Dimensions of Indian History Revisited



Prof. Kousik Sastri

pencil

ISBN 978-93-5610-210-1

Published in India 2022 by Pencil

*A brand of*
One Point Six Technologies Pvt. Ltd.
123, Building J2, Shram Seva Premises,
Wadala Truck Terminal, Wadala (E)
Mumbai 400037, Maharashtra, INDIA
**E** connect@thepencilapp.com
**W** www.thepencilapp.com

# Author biography

Poet, writer, novelist, non fiction writer and retired professor

CONTENTS

# Tipu Sultan and Mysorean Rocket

If only the 'rocket' is mentioned, then yes, this thing was first built in India during the time of Tipu Sultan i.e. at the very end of the eighteenth century. However, the rocket is mentioned in the history of other parts of the world long before this. For example, in the eleventh century, the first mention of gunpowder and volcanic arrows was found in the Chinese war science book Yujing Zhangyao. This is considered to be the earliest form of rocket science in the history of civilization. According to the traveler Avalia Chelebi, in the 17th century, in the year 1733, Lyari Hassan Chelebi launched a rocket in Istanbul at the birth of the daughter of Sultan Murad IV of the Ottoman Empire. However, there is disagreement over this incident. Due to the lack of detailed information and exaggerated descriptions, it is considered as a legend without science. Therefore, considering the definite history, the rocket of Tipu Sultan's period can be considered as the first used rocket in the world. However, this rocket has nothing to do with the manned space rocket (although both use Newton's third law as a principle). Tipu Sultan's rocket was very small - the size of a spear used in the battle of Mysore against the British.

# Why is it called 'Bharatvarsha' and not Bharat

The same word has different meanings in Sanskrit. The money has to be recovered according to the context in which it was used. This is difficult for researchers in many cases, but it is quite interesting. However, the word year (IAST: varṣ a) also has different meanings. And it has been used in many different ways in different contexts. It has to do with rainfall. Rain means rain, but also rain of something else. In most parts of India, it rains once a year, so the year is also referred to as the year. There is a rainy season so that - one year. Again, people knew that rain is associated with mountains. A mountain can contain rain. That is why the mountain was also called year or year mountain or parvat barsha.. For the same reason, the cloud was also called the barsha. Important in this answer is the word 'barsha' which is synonymous with mountain. These mountains cause rainfall, on top of that, these mountains divide the land into different parts. Now those divided parts are also called years. The mountains that cause rainfall are also called rain mountains (barṣ aparbata). There are six / seven such mountains in the year- Snowy year Hemkutvarsha New Year Blue year White year Horny year or Horny year Polar years Not only did these monsoons bring rain, they also divided the land into different parts. Since those divisions are made by the mountain of the year, the year would be at the end of the name of these divisions. The terrain divided by this monsoon is- Diamond Year Happy New Year Ilavartvarsh Harivarsha Ketumalvarsha (separated in Monier-Williams - Ketuvarsha and Malvarsha, no mention of next year.) Kimpurushvarsha Good year Kinnarvarsha India This is the mystery of the name "year". May be made for fantasy. It is mentioned in Vishnu Purana- North Jatsamudrasya: Himadreshchaib South. Year Tad Bharatang Name: Bharati Yatra Santatih. [Translation: The year north of the sea, south of the snow mountain, the year is called Bharatvarsha, where the descendants of Bharata live.] I have received the name "Kimpurushvarsha" many times in Buddhist literature and in modern works following it. By this was meant Tibet. India's relationship with Tibet is very ancient. The Tibetan king also invaded India once during or before the Palshas rule in Bengal. However, that is not the subject of discussion. The Mahabharata speaks of victory by Arjuna, the Kimburusvarsha under Kubera. And it is said that in the northern hemisphere of Kinnarvarsha.

# The Real Story of Shahjahan and Mamtaj

The love story of Emperor Shahjahan and Mumtaz is one of the most popular love stories in the world. There are many more immortal love stories like these. However, the love story of Emperor Shahjahan and Mumtaz has aroused response for a special reason. That is the famous Taj Mahal built by Emperor Shah Jahan for Mumtaz. Today we will highlight the details of the Taj Mahal here. Brief story of love between Emperor Shahjahan and Mumtaz: The time was 1812 AD. Emperor Shah Jahan was then 20 years old. One day, while passing through the market of Agra, suddenly Shahjahan's eyes went to a beautiful girl. The girl named Arjumand Begum is 15 years old. Shahjahan liked Arjumand Begum at first sight. Later, on May 10, 1812, Mumtaz married Prince Khurram (Emperor Shahjahan). (But Wikipedia states that they were both 15 and 14 years old at the time of marriage). Earlier, Emperor Shah Jahan married a Persian princess for political reasons. Later, Emperor Shah Jahan changed the name of his wife to Mumtaz Mahal. Mumtaz was Shah Jahan's favorite Begum. In her nineteen years of marriage, Mumtaz had a total of fourteen children. Mumtaz Mahal died in 1831 at the age of 39 after giving birth to her 14th child. In the grief of losing his wife, Muhyman Shahjahan built this wonderful symbol of love for the memory of his beloved wife. For seven days and nights after the death of his wife, Shahjahan did not eat anything. He did not leave the house. After seven days Shahjahan came out. Then his hair color turned gray, and face pale.

The love story of Emperor Shahjahan and Mumtaz is as much talked about as Mumtaz is actually the wife of Emperor Shahjahan. According to Wikipedia, Mumtaz was the second wife of Emperor Shah Jahan. Somewhere it is said to be the 3rd wife of Mumtaz Shahjahan, somewhere it is said to be the 4th wife. In fact, the exact number of wives is not stated anywhere. Controversy over the love story of Emperor Shahjahan and Mumtaz: A professor named PN Oak also questioned the veracity of Shahjahan and Mumtaz's love story in his "Taj Mahal: The True Story". In his writings, he mentions that the love story of Mumtaz and Shahjahan is basically a fairy tale which is created in folklore. Because such a deep and wonderful love is not mentioned in any official document or text of India at that time. He presented some more documentaries which proved that the Taj Mahal never belonged to Emperor Shah Jahan. Among them is Marvin Miller, an archaeologist from New York, who examined the walls of the Taj Mahal on the banks of the river Jamuna. He got the information from his carbon test that this carbon is 300 years older than the reign of Emperor Shah Jahan! Another thing is that a European tourist visited Agra in 1838. The time is only 7 years after the death of Shahjahan's wife Mumtaz. But he did not mention the Taj Mahal in his book Travels to India.

The debate continues: The love story of Emperor Shahjahan and Mumtaz says that Emperor Shahjahan saw

Mumtaz in the market and liked Mumtaz at the first sight. But it is also heard that Mumtaz was married before she got married to Shahjahan and Emperor Shahjahan killed Mumtaz's husband and then married Mumtaz. Not only that, before Mumtaz, Emperor Shahjahan had 3 more wives and after marrying Mumtaz, Emperor Shahjahan got married three more times. Even after Mumtaz's death, Shahjahan married Mumtaz's own younger sister. The name of the designer of the Taj Mahal was Isha Mohammad. He made a sculpture to give as a gift to his wife. Later, due to the choice of Emperor Shah Jahan, the world-famous Taj Mahal was built in the style of that design and the person's eyes were destroyed so that he could not create this design again. Not only that, the twenty thousand workers who worked day and night to build this palace were also cut off by Emperor Shah Jahan. Behind the cruel and brutal history of love lies the love story of Emperor Shahjahan-Mumtaz and behind the Taj Mahal.

# Indian Thugs

The word thagi originates from the Sanskrit word thug, meaning deceiver, deceiver. Thug is one of the words that was added to the English language during the rule of India. The word means thief or robber. The word thag comes from the Sanskrit word thagi. The story of the thugs gained popularity in 1839 through Philip Meadows Taylor's novel Confessions of a Thug, and at the same time the word 'thug' became part of the English language. In Bengali, thugi refers to a special class of bandits who would kill a passer-by with a yellow handkerchief or cloth wrapped around his neck. Cruel and cunning murderers like thugs are rare in history. The thugs were first known in 1358 in the book 'History of Firoz Shah' written by the historian Ziauddin Barani. . The thugs established a reign of terror in Bengal and northern India in the 13th to 19th centuries. In fact, they have been carrying on this activity for many centuries. They arrived in Bengal around 1290. After some thugs were caught during the Sultan's reign around 1290, some say the number was one thousand, they were taken to New Delhi but the Sultan did not kill any of them but ordered them to be sent by boat to the lower country so that they would never again create chaos in Delhi. Can't Sir SM Elliott, "History of India" And since then, this murderous group has spread in the waters, lands and fields of Bengal. This is probably the beginning of the history of thugs in Bengal. How to kill: The thugs used a yellow handkerchief about 30 inches long to kill. He folded the handkerchief and tied two silver coins on its two heads. At the time of the murder, there were three thugs trying to kill one of them. After killing the thugs, they would bury the bodies in the ground. If anyone escaped, the thugs would kill them. They did not usually kill beggars, musicians, dancers, sweepers, oil sellers, carpenters, blacksmiths, cripples, lepers, Ganges carriers and women. For hundreds of years, countless travelers were lost in different parts of India. Where, how to lose, no one knew. As if by some magic they could be erased from the bosom of the earth. How many people lost in this way? According to the Guinness Book of World Records 20 million!

Suppression: At first, the British rulers considered the disappearance of a pilgrim as an isolated incident, but as the British gradually began to disappear, Governor-General Lord Bentinck learned that religious extremists were involved. He then instructed William Henry Schliemann, administrator of India in 1830, to eradicate the thugs. From the introduction to Colonel Sliman's masterpiece, it is clear that the attitude of the English magistrates was as daring as that of the thugs: The intensive plan adopted by the British government to suppress the thugs soon began to bear fruit.

Muslim thugs used to start worshiping Bhabani in the same way. They believed that if worshiping Bhabani was unwelcome to God, it would not go away for so many years, surely there would be some terrible evil. Although they practiced the Muslim religion in their personal lives, they followed the rules and regulations of Bhabani. The thugs used to communicate among themselves in various sign languages, calling it 'Ramosi'. The word 'jhirni' was used to describe the preparation for killing and the word 'tamaku lao' or 'pan lao' to kill. As soon as this instruction was received, a noose was tied around the victim's neck. The Sothas were at the forefront, identifying potential victims and gathering information about the victims. Those who watched the movement were called 'Tilhai', they were a little behind the team. The Nisars were responsible for setting up tents in safe places. The thugs had a structure of professional division of labor on the basis of different roles and skills. The team members were given very specific responsibilities. He was responsible for the construction of the tomb which was called 'Will'. The one who held the prey was called 'chamochi'. It is the responsibility of the "kisser" to hold the hand so that the victim does not interrupt. The 'kiss' will push the victim's legs and throw him to the ground. 'Bhojara' will take the corpses to the grave. The responsibility of 'kuthawa' is to break the knees of the bodies, fold them with the chin and bury them. Those in charge of guarding the corpses and alerting them when they smelled danger were called 'Furkadena'. The Furzanas were responsible for clearing the area of the killings. A feast of nectar of thugs sitting on the graves of newly dead people. That feast is nothing but a feast of molasses. Whenever he found a lone traveler, he would gladly invite him to travel with the group. According to them, once one eats this molasses, he will become a swindler.

# Naga Queen Guidinliu

Everyone has participated in the independence movement irrespective of race, religion and caste. No one has made the ultimate sacrifice. Again, someone has dedicated himself to the service of the country even after the country became independent. One such heroine is Queen Gaidinliu. Who was a Naga spiritual and political leader. Queen Guidinleu was born on January 26, 1915 in the village of Nunkao in Manipur. At the age of thirteen, Guidinliu joined the Heraka religious movement with his half-brother, Hypu Jadonang. It was originally a religious movement of the Naga tribes which later took the form of an anti-British movement. The local Zheliangrang tribe became her followers. Hypo Jadonang was later arrested and hanged by police. Guidinliu then forbade the Naga tribes to pay taxes to the British and called for the liberation of Manipur and the local Naga inhabited areas from British rule. Gaidinliu started a fierce movement to defend the right to Naga autonomy. The government ordered his arrest. She then evaded the police and went into hiding in different villages of Assam and Manipur. Guidinliu then moved to the village of Pulomi. There her followers started building a fort. But suddenly the Assam Rifles soldiers launched a surprise attack there. Guidinliu was caught. She was sent to Imphal. She was sentenced to life imprisonment. Guidinliu was imprisoned in Shillong, Guwahati, Aizawl, Tura and other places. Jaharlal Nehru met her while she was in prison. He called Guidinleu the queen of the mountains. Gaidinliu was later released when India became independent. But she could not return to her village until 1952. Later, Naga separatist groups also began to oppose Gaidinliu. Her Heraka religious movement also continued to be in conflict. The Naga Baptist Church declared the Heraka movement to be anti-Christian. Guidinliu wanted to form a separate Zheliangrong district. She went into hiding in retaliation for the proposed separate government of the Naga organizations and formed her own armed forces and parallel administrative divisions. After a long struggle, she returned to the mainstream in 1966. Guidinliu went to Kohima and met with Prime Minister Lal Bahadur Shastri, demanding a separate Zheliangrang division. Then, on September 24 of that year, Guidinliu's forces surrendered. In Kohima (nineteen hundred and seventy-two) she was awarded a copper plate in honor of the freedom struggle. Gaidinliu was awarded the Padma Bhushan in 1982. She also received the Vivekananda Seva Award. In 1991, Queen Guidinleu returned to her native Lanka. There, on February 17, 1979, at the age of seventy-eight, this great freedom fighter died.

# Kohinoor, the Cursed Diamond

A gem rich in history. Diamonds. His name is Kohinoor. It is an oval white diamond. The current weight is 105 carats (21.6 grams) or 319 ounces. Initially the weight was 656 carats. The weight of the Kohinoor was tested at the royal court of Shah Jahan. French jeweler Tavarnia checked and found that he weighed a little over 26 carats. Hortensio Georges, a Venetian diamond cutter, was the first to cut the diamond with an incompetent hand. Emperor Shah Jahan fined him 10,000 rupees for such a great fault. Kohinoor has never been traded. It has 33 sides. At various times the diamond was in the possession of Hindu, Persian, Mughal, Turkish, Afghan, Sikh and British rulers. According to Sir Wolf, the Kohinoor was ruled by the Mughals for 213 years, the Afghans for 6 years and the British for 126 years by 2011. The diamond was mined in the twelfth century from the Kallar mine at Kallar village in the Hindu-dominated Santoshnagar area of Guntar district in Andhra Pradesh, India. At the same time the twin Darya-i-Nur of Kohinoor was also lifted. This diamond is known to be in one of the oldest manuscripts, The person under this diamond will rule the world. But in the end the ultimate misfortune will come down in his life. The scripture also says that only gods or women will be free from this curse. This diamond first came to the possession of the Malwa dynasty in the south. After extraction from the mine, it was handed over to the Malwa dynasty. But for a long time they could not keep it to themselves. The Malwa king was defeated and ruthlessly killed in a battle with the neighboring Kakatiya kings. And then this diamond came under the Kakatiya king. Then this precious gem was in the possession of the Kakatiya kings but its durability was very short. The Kakatiya kings placed the diamond as the eye of the goddess in a temple in the capital Barangal and thought that no one would find this diamond. But by then the beauty of this diamond had spread abroad. Then the rule of Khilji dynasty in Delhi came to an end. The reign of the Turkish ruler Ghiyasuddin Tughlaq Shah began. Knowing the diversity of this diamond, he tried to claim it. In 1323, he declared war on Pratap Rudra, king of Kakatiya, and sent his loyal and cunning general Ulugh Khan to defeat Pratap Rudra. Ulugh Khan's initial attack was repulsed, but he was soon defeated by the unprepared army of the Kakatiya kingdom. King Pratap Rudra lost his life in this surprise battle. Looting and destruction continued for a month in Barangal, the capital of Kakatiya state. Hundreds of diamonds, jewels, silver, jewels were looted and sent to Delhi which contained the cursed diamond. Change hands again Over time, the diamond became the property of Turkish ruler Ibrahim Lodi. He was the ruler of Delhi till 1525 AD. At this time Mughal Emperor Babur declared war on Ibrahim Lodi with the aim of conquering India. King Vikramaditya of Gwalior sided with Ibrahim Lodi in this battle. Ibrahim Lodi was defeated in this battle of Pani Path and later Ibrahim Lodi was killed by one of his loyal soldiers. After this battle Humayun Ibrahim, son of Babar, entered the palace of Lodi. The family of Ibrahim Lodi and King Vikramaditya were staying in this palace at that time. Humayun enters the palace and assures the weeping women that they will be treated as they deserve. On hearing this from Humayun, Ibrahim Lodi's mother Sonali handed over a box to Humayun. Humayun opened the box and saw a diamond. From this time the rights of diamonds passed into the hands of Mughal emperors. Due to the irony of fate, sultanate rights were not established on the throne of Delhi. Is he under the curse of diamonds? After the debate. Behind the destruction of the Mughals when diamonds Then this diamond came into the hands of the Mughals. But did they manage to control themselves in that diamond, or did their lives go downhill? We will know that from the next story. History continued to repeat itself even during the Mughal period. When this diamond came to Babar, Babar was sitting on the throne of Delhi. But not for long. Babar died of a disease. After that Humayun came in possession of diamonds and masnad of Delhi. But the kingdom of Delhi did not last long. He retaliated and constantly struggled to restore his lost kingdom. All life he had to wander like a nomad, to spend life on the battlefield. Later, Humayun got back the Mansad of Delhi with the help of Emperor Shah Tamasp of Persia. In gratitude, Emperor Humayun presented the diamond to Shah. Mansad of Delhi got back but the diamond was lost. So far the curse of diamonds has been steady and the Mughals have been ruling India almost smoothly. After Humayun's death, the rights of Delhi came to Akbar. They did not have this diamond during the reign of Emperor Akbar and his son Emperor Jahangir. In 1757, Jahangir's son Emperor Shah Jahan received the diamond as a gift from the diamond merchant Mir Jumla. Shah Jahan was the one who talked about Kohinoor the most. Shahjahan used the diamond on his peacock throne. One hundred years later, the curse of diamonds came back. The beginning is the history of the destruction of the Mughal Empire. When Shahjahan fell ill, his four sons became embroiled in a civil war over inheritance. One of his sons, Aurangzeb, defeated all his brothers and captured the masnad of Delhi. Shahjahan was captured in the fort of Agra and diedDuring the Jeb, the Mughal Empire began to collapse. When the Mughal Empire was on the verge of disintegration and destruction, Nadir Shah was invited to help bring back the glorious days of Muslim rule. But he was cheated without paying the promised money. Nadir Shah of Persia invaded India and looted this Kohinoor diamond with peacock throne. But his fate did not last long. On June 19, 1848, the Persian emperor Nadir Shah died in his sleep at the hands of an assassin. Change hands again Nadir Shah Afghan General Ahmed Shah Durrani strategically took possession of the diamond. Diamonds later came to Suja Shah Durrani, the ruler of Afghanistan. In 1830, after being defeated by the defeated King Ahmed Shah of Afghanistan, Shah Shuja fled to Lahore with the Kohinoor. Durrani's family was not spared from the curse of diamonds. Shah Shuja handed over the diamond to Sikh Maharaja Ranjit Singh of Punjab. In return, Ranjit Singh restored the throne of Afghanistan to Shah Suja. Ranjit Singh knew about the curse of this diamond. So he dedicated this diamond to Jagannath temple. But destiny is very cruel. After the death of Ranjit Singh, the English seeking his kingdom wanted to take advantage of the chaos in the state. After the death of Ranjit Singh, the Punjabi throne passed through four different rulers in four years. At the end of the violent period, the only people who stood up for the throne were younger son Dilip Singh and his mother, Rani Jindan. And in 1849, after capturing Jindan after the Second Anglo-Sikh War, the British forced Dilip to sign a legal document amending the Lahore Agreement, demanding that Dilip be granted Kohinoor and claim sovereignty. The boy was only 10 years old then. The Kohinoor fell into the hands of the British before Jagannath was crowned. Diamonds in the hands of the British The diamond was snatched from the hands of Dilip Singh, the minor son of Ranjit Singh, who was defeated by the British. Thus one of their most valuable resources is lost from the subcontinent. Lord Dalhousie handed the diamond to Queen Victoria on behalf of the East India Company in 1850. The ship HMS Medea, on which the diamond was shipped to England, was also hit by a series of disasters. Five people, including FM Lawrence, the ship's second-in-command, died of cholera on the voyage. By now everyone understood that the precious curse was the most talked about diamond in the history of the name 'Kohinoor'. Whenever a man holds it, it is destroyed. The only exception is women. Women have always survived its curse. No member of the British royal family kept the diamond with them. It has always been in the possession of the queens.

# India's first armed freedom fighter

In an effort to drive the British out of the country, a man first consciously took up arms. He was the first armed freedom fighter of India. Her name is Basudev Balvant Pharke. A severe famine occurred in Maharashtra as a result of the British government's policy of exploitation and oppression. And the British government adopted blindness as its only policy. Lots of people die of disease and starvation. However, the British government does not give any shortcomings in the collection of rent. Forcible collection of rent continues. Some wealthy merchants sided with the British for their own benefit, and even in times of great famine, they locked up warehouses to sell food grains at higher prices. Basudev became very angry and devoted himself to the cause of building a British free India. He himself learned to wield a sword, ride a horse, and wield a gun. The local Koli, Veel and Dhangar tribes formed a revolutionary party of 300 people. The group looted various warehouses and distributed the stored food grains among the famine-stricken people. The British government's various rent collection and savings centers were also attacked by this group. He looted millions of rupees and used it to serve the famine-stricken people. He liberated the city of Pune from British rule for a few days. And because of this, and because of the constant looting, his name became infamous in London as well. The British rulers called him a "robber" and made repeated attempts to apprehend him. He used to hide in the forest from village to village to prevent being caught. The British government set a price of Rs 1 lakh on his head to catch him. He set the counter-bomb on the governor's head at Rs 1 lakh. He determined the reward for killing a European. He is not only famous for looting. He set up the Pune Native Institution in Pune in 180, which was later transformed into the Maharashtra Shiksha Sangstha. He also set up a school to promote education among the country's boys. A villager reported the incident to British police, who arrested him on July 20, 1879, after a duel. He was tried in Pune. And since no evidence was gathered against him, the British administration sentenced him to life imprisonment, citing his own diary as evidence. Realizing that it was not safe to keep him in the country, the administration transferred him (to present-day Yemen) to a prison in the city of Aden. It is said that on February 13, 183, he broke down the prison door empty-handed and escaped. But he was soon caught. On February 17, he went on a hunger strike. Several episodes of the famous novel "Ananda Math" by the literary emperor Bankimchandra Chattopadhyay are inspired by the life of Basudev Balwant Pharak. Due to the objections of the British administration, he reduced the events inspired by Farak's life by changing the events to prevent the book from being banned in the next 5 editions. This great man was the first to embark on a direct armed struggle against the foreign British rulers and he was an inspiration to many. Today he is immortal because of his fame.

# In the time of Emperor Ashoka, a secret society consisting of nine people

Emperor Ashoka Maurya was born in 304 BC. Emperor Ashoka was the son of Bindusara and Dharma and the grandson of Chandragupta Maurya, the founder of the Maurya Empire. Ashoka was a follower of Vedic religion in his early life. His reign was from 298 to 262 BC. From the time he became king, Ashoka focused on expanding his empire. He annexed present-day Assam and Bangladesh in the east, Iran and Afghanistan in the west, and almost the whole of southern India in the north from the Pamir Glands in the north. Ashoka then set out to occupy the Kalinga Republic, which his ancestors had never conquered. In 261 BC (263 BC, a fierce battle took place near the Dhauli hills on the banks of the river Daya). Emperor Ashoka's army killed about one lakh Kalinga warriors and about one and a half lakh villagers. It is known from history that even after winning this war, Emperor Ashoka did not have peace in his mind. Rather, he became more confused by its horror. This quarrel doesn't bring anything good, Raktaganga gives in the book - this thought made Ashok mourn. Seeing the horrors of the Kalinga war, Ashoka took an oath not to fight for the rest of his life. Emperor Ashoka was initiated into Buddhism. He started preaching Buddhism all over India.

He also started preaching in Malay, Sinhala and Indonesia. His teachings on Buddhism later spread to China, Nepal and Mongolia. The battle-loving warrior king transformed himself into a peace-loving non-violent man. Emperor Ashoka's empire was vast. He ruled over almost the entire Indian subcontinent, excluding the Hindu Kush, ie, Assam to the east of Afghanistan, and the Pamirs to the north and a small part of the south. The emperor felt that knowledge was the most powerful. The effectiveness of the research, which should be used for the benefit of human society, if it falls into the hands of incompetent or dishonest people, would be extremely detrimental to human society as a whole. Emperor Ashoka instructed these nine persons to record the research of certain special subjects in symbolic form or in sign language formulas which would not be able to reach any other person outside. The symbolic knowledge or research source of that 'unknown person' was kept with utmost secrecy. In 1923 (according to some, 1926), Talbot Mundy, a 25-year-old British police officer in Calcutta, published a series of novels about the "unknown man" in Adventure Magazine. The name of the novel was 'The Nine Unknown'. Historians Louis Powell and Jacques Bergier later researched the subject and wrote in their book about Emperor Ashoka: God is pleased with man's generosity and great deeds, that was the teaching of Ashoka. All living beings have the right to live in peace and happiness. Ashoka preached these through his words and deeds. Ashoka formed an association with some people nearby to complete his work. The work of this association was how to keep people away from bad deeds, how to live together without harming others. However, it was not possible for Ashoka to see everything at once. Since he had a huge responsibility to govern the state, Ashoka entrusted this task to nine wise and virtuous men of India. The names of the nine were never released for security reasons. An association of gems, not unknown to Emperor Ashoka, was formed. " Starting from nature, psychology, the branch in which as much knowledge as possible can be acquired, began to take from all these nine people. If ordinary people knew about this science, they would not call it anything but destruction - thinking that they would not even propagate it. Ashoka gave them the opportunity and permission to roam in all fields of scientific theory, information and technology. It was everyone's responsibility to write a special book in which they were proficient. From time to time they would change, enlarge and refine them. But here's the thing. If someone could not finish the book entrusted to him, then the responsibility of the book would go to the next successor. In this case, the number of members of the association would not be increased. The number nine was kept constant. If you are suffering from a disease, or if you are dying, or if you want to voluntarily give up your responsibilities, you are cordially invited. But he had to swear that he would not reveal his name and his deeds to anyone. It is believed that the lifespan of this unknown Navaratna association is about two thousand years. It is said that Emperor Ashoka was aware of the horrors of war; So he wanted people not to use their intelligence for bad things. During his reign, science was practiced with great secrecy. This privacy practice continues to this day. From the end of the last century, intimate association with different secret societies of different scientists from different countries came out in large numbers. The bloody journey of history is not just about war, love and disaster; Many of its journeys are deeply intertwined with the practice of science.

## Why is India not a father but a mother

Not only India but almost all the countries of the world call their country as motherland or motherland. The exceptions are Germany, Denmark, Iceland, Norway, Sweden, Netherlands, Austria, Switzerland and Belarus. They call their country fatherland. And our country has been considered as mother since ancient times. And in our religion-society-culture, mother has been given a place above father. Where the father is equal to the heavens and before the gods - "Father heaven, father religion, father paramang tapa. Pitori Pritima Panne Priyante Sarva Devatah. " And the mother has been given a place in heaven and above - "Janani Janmabhumishch Swargadapi Gariyasi". And not just the RSS or the masses, it must be remembered that the first picture of Bharatmata was drawn by Abanindranath Tagore. Hopefully no one will call him a pagan. And it is not a paganism to personify an ideal!

# Why Khulna is in Pakistan

Even after Khulna became Hindu majority, Khulna was included in Pakistan for various logical reasons. However, there is a big misconception among the Hindus of West Bengal about Khulna. Despite being a Hindu majority, Khulna came to Pakistan mainly for two reasons: Geographical: The Hindu-Muslim ratio in Khulna was 51:49. However, out of 3 subdivisions of Khulna, two subdivisions on both sides (Satkhira, Bagerhat) were Muslim majority. And in the middle Khulna there were more Hindus. In this case, if the whole Khulna was added to India for only one subdivision, then two Muslim subdivisions would fall in India. Even if Khulna was given to Pakistan through Bagerhat Pakistan on the eastern side, there would be trouble with Satkhira. RELIGIOUS: Considering the Hindu-Muslim background behind the partition of Bengal, confusion arises in some cases. Although there was not much political division among the Muslims of Bengal, the Hindus were divided into two branches. Although caste Hindus wanted to join Bengal or India, another group of Hindus, who were known as Scheduled Caste or Dalit Hindus or Scheduled Caste, did not want to go to India. In undivided Bengal, their MLAs supported the Muslim League government. In continuation of this they also supported Pakistan movement. Proof of this is that in the first cabinet of independent Pakistan, the scheduled leader Jogendranath Mandal was the law minister (1947-50). Now let's talk about Khulna. A large section of the Hindus in Khulna were Scheduled Hindus who wanted to join Pakistan. As a result, with a large number of Scheduled Castes supporting Pakistan, including 49% Muslims, the pro-Indians became a minority in Khulna. As a result, the inclusion of Khulna in Pakistan was logical. Also, according to some, to save the port of Calcutta, Murshidabad, the district of about 80% Muslims, the majority of the Muslim-majority Maldah district (excluding Chapainawabganj) for the convenience of Northeast India, the Muslim-majority Nadia and Dinajpur districts and Jessore's Banagram subdivision "As Khulna was included in Pakistan.

## the first to introduce spiritual India to Europe and the United States

India's first 'spiritual ambassador' On August 15, 183, ten years before the Chicago Religious Conference, a ship called the Marathon came to a halt in Boston, USA. A 43-year-old Bengali was on that ship. His aim was to propagate the traditional spiritualism of India in America. However, he had earlier completed his tour of England and Germany in 184 for the same purpose. And five years after that visit, he began to think about preaching in the United States. Therefore, the first honor of India's 'spiritual ambassador' to the West is not Vivekananda, he deserves it. He also attended the Chicago Religious Conference of 1893. At that time he represented Brahmanism. He was even elected a member of the Advisory Council of the Chicago Congress of Religions. Find out what Dr. Henry Burroughs, the president of the executive committee, said about the purpose of this meeting. According to him, the meeting was aimed at consolidating brotherhood between different religions and exploring the characteristics of each religion. Who is he? The man's name is Pratap Chandra Majumdar. Born in Hughli on 2 October 1840, he was educated in Calcutta. He studied first at Hair School and later at Presidency College. In 1859, when he was only 19, he came in contact with Brahmanism. He got acquainted with Maharshi Debendranath Tagore and Keshab Chandra Sen. After that it did not take long for him to be initiated into Brahmanism. After his conversion, he became actively involved in religious preaching and became known as a close follower of Keshab Chandra Sen. He was once in the Bank of Bengal during his career. He also got Keshab Chandra Sen as a colleague there. The first target is Europe By that time the English translation of the Bhagavad Gita had reached some parts of Europe and the people of Europe had become acquainted with Indian spiritualism. He traveled to Europe in 184 with the help of the Unitarian Church. Encouraged by that success, the proposal to travel the world at the annual festival of the Brahmo Samaj in January 183 was accepted and he was allowed to represent abroad on behalf of the Navavidhan Samaj. At the same time a fundraising committee was formed. Within two months of the proposal, Pratap Chandra traveled to London. He left on March 12 and reached there on April 24. The British and Foreign Unitarian Association was in charge of his visit. And the editor of the original entrepreneurial company is Robert Spears himself. Pratap Chandra used to speak in various meetings there. And enough people came to hear that speech. Somewhere even senior missionaries were present. Three thousand people gathered at Birmingham Town Hall for his meeting. During this time he spoke in Scotland, Ireland and Wales, in addition to England. The goal this time is America It was during this period that he came to Boston. Concord from there. His first speech at a public meeting at Emerson Hall was well attended. He then spoke in Saratoga. In the beginning he used to chant

Sanskrit mantras and sometimes observed a minute of silence. This style of serving was eye-catching. Pratap Chandra could speak excellent English. Paper began to be written praising that English. He was described as a traveling Hindu philosopher, teacher and reformer in the East. He is said to have been better able to speak than many national leaders, generals, and clergy in the United States. In this way the people of India became interested in the religious reforms. Encouraged by his success, the American Unitarian Association came forward. In 1893, his book, The Oriental Christ, was published, which was well-received in the United States. Publishers Geo H. Ellis, Franklin Street, Boston. In October of that year, he was elected a member of the American Antiquarian Society. Hindu Protestant It is worth mentioning here that one of the major reasons for Pratap Chandra Majumdar's popularity abroad is that people started thinking of him as a preacher of Christianity. And because of this he had to go through a lot of difficult situations. However, he opposed him. Instead, Pratap Chandra referred to himself as a Hindu Protestant. According to him, Protestants have appeared in Hinduism as well as in Christianity through the ages. For example, Sikhism, Vaishnavism or Brahma. A book written by Pratapchand Madjumdar Pratap Chandra Majumdar wrote several books. Some of them are 'The Oriental Christ', 'The Life and Teaching of Keshab Chandra Sen', 'Will the Brahmo Samaj Last?', 'Heart Beats', 'The Spirit of God', 'The Faith and Progress of the Brahmo Samaj'. 'Etc. Debate There is a controversy over Pratap Chandra's notoriety and propaganda against Vivekananda in Chicago in 1893. It is not our intention to judge his truth. However, it must be admitted that Pratap

Chandra Majumdar of Calcutta was a pioneer in propagating Indian spiritualism across the Atlantic.

# Taimur's Barbarity in India

During the reign of Nasiruddin Muhammad Shah, the last ruler of the Tughlaq dynasty, the military leader of Samarkand, Taimur Long / Long or Amir Taimur, invaded India in 1396 AD. Taimur Long was born in 1338 in the city of Ķech in Samarkand, Central Asia. Timur Long's father, Amir Targhi Barla, belonged to the Surgan or Chaghtai Turkish community of the Turkish tribes. He was the ruler of a small region called Ketch. After the death of his father in 1389, at the age of 33, he ascended the throne of the kingdom of Kech. One of Timur's legs was stabbed during a childhood battle. From this time on he began to walk limping. This is why the word "Long" is associated with his name. He established his authority in Central Asia and the wider region of Asia. Timur Long became famous in the history of the world by conquering Mesopotamia, Persia, Syria, Turkey, Asia Minor and Afghanistan. Timur Long then decided to invade India. The purpose of Timur's expedition to India: From Timur Long's autobiography "Tuzuk e Taimuri (Milfuza e Taimuri)" it is known that Timur Long's expedition to India had two objectives. (1) To convert the Indians who are obsessed with polytheism and paganism to the true religion and (2) to plunder the immense wealth of India. In fact, his sole purpose was to plunder the vast wealth of India. The destruction of paganism is just an excuse. When his army and Amir Umrah objected to his expedition to such a distance from Central Asia, he raised the issue of religion with them. In this context, Dr. Majumdar writes - "As a matter of fact, he combined in himself the savage ferocity of Ceinghiz Khan and the fanaticism of Sultan Mahmud." Description of Taimur Long's invasion of India: In early 1396 AD, Pir Muhammad Multan, the ancestor of Taimur, captured it. In April of that year, Taimur Long crossed the Indus, Jhilam and Ravi rivers with a large army from Samarkand and marched towards the capital Delhi. He appeared on the outskirts of Delhi on 12 December 1396, plundering Dipalpur, Bhatnar, Shirsa, Kaithal and killing many men and women. About one lakh people were killed here. Sultan Nasiruddin Mohammad of Delhi and his prime minister Mallu Iqbal set out to resist him on 16 December 1396. Defeated by Taimur Long, Mallu Iqbal fled to Baran province and Sultan Nasiruddin Muhammad to Gujarat. Then he entered Delhi and on 16 December 1396, Taimur and his army carried out looting and killing for 15 long days. The Jain historian writes that Timur's army rejoiced at the construction of the monument to the Hindus. The carcasses became the food of carnivorous animals and birds. He then returned to the country in 1399 AD with great wealth and innumerable prisoners. On his way back to the country he plundered the areas of Firozabad, Meerut, Haridwar and Jammu. Before leaving India, he appointed Khizir Khan as ruler of Multan, Lahore and Dipalpur on 7 March 1399. On 19 March 1399, Taimur Long crossed the Indus and returned to the country. Impact of Timur Long's invasion of India: The impact of Timur Long's invasion of India is important in the political and economic life of India. As a result of the plunder of Taimur Long, a lot of gold, silver, gems and pearls went abroad from India. Historian Badauni writes that those who were rescued from Timur lost their lives in a natural disaster and as a result the population of Delhi was so reduced that not a single bird was seen flying in the skies of Delhi for two months. With millions of people, cattle are ruined. The invasion of India by Taimur Long revealed the plight of the military forces of the Sultanate. After the invasion of India by Taimur Long, independent states were formed in the territories of Gujarat, Samana, Biyana, Kalpi, Mahaba, Multan, Punjab and Indus. The Sultani Empire shrunk from Delhi to the small border of Palam. Taimur Long brutally persecuted Hindus in the name of religion. As a result, communal strife arose among Hindus and Muslims. Hindu parents are terrified and start giving child marriages to their daughters. Because it seems to be one of the ways to protect the dignity of women. This inevitably has an adverse effect on society. Taimur Long's army destroyed many buildings and temples. He also brought back many skilled Indian artisans, masons and artists. India was deprived of the contribution of their talents and Samarkand art flourished. Through all these Indian artists, the trend of Indian art spread to various parts of Central Asia. After the invasion of India by Taimur Long, Nasiruddin Muhammad Shah returned to Delhi from Gujarat and ruled over as little territory as possible. The dominion of the Delhi Sultan was then confined to the areas of Delhi, Rotak, Doab and Sambal. When Nasiruddin Mohammad Shah died in 1413, the Umrahs of Delhi installed an Afghan Umrah named

Daulat Khan Lodi on the throne. This marked the end of two hundred years of Turkish rule in India.

# History of Kalapani

Standing in the scorching sun and working inhumanely for six hours straight, Sushil Dasgupta's hands are stained with his own blood. At the same rate, his whole body was sweating as he worked incessantly to break the coconut and extract the fiber from its husk. The throat is dry and has become wood. He stopped work for a moment and asked the guard to give him a glass of water. The water didn't match, but a new brutal game started with the guards' face-to-face remarks. Sushil, who was wearing handcuffs, was told to walk and fetch water for everyone from the nearby river. As he walked some distance through the thorny forest, a stream of blood flowed from his weary body. Sushil lost consciousness and remained there. Not even a sip of water was added to his forehead like last time. Numerous political prisoners like Sushil have lost their lives while working in such an inhuman environment. Under the British colonial rule, potentially young people who could stand up against colonialism were sent to the Andaman Cellular Jail in the Andaman and Nicobar Islands near the Bay of Bengal as punishment. To the common people, the jail is better known as 'Kalapani'. The word 'kala' here means death, and as it is situated on the shores of the Bay of Bengal, the name is associated with 'water'. Kalapani or Cellular Jail is a former prison located in the Andaman Islands of India. The construction of this prison was completed in 1906. Many prominent activists of the Indian independence movement like Batukeshwar Dutt, Ullaskar Dutt and Binayak Damodar Savarkar were kept in this jail. Now this building is being used as a national memorial. The only cellular gel in the Andaman Islands is made of terracotta brick. Kalapani was one of the infamous prisons set up during the British rule in India, especially to hold the anti-British revolutionaries in Bengal. Prominent protesters and activists like Batukeshwar Dutt, Ullaskar Dutt, Binayak Damodar Savarkar who participated in the Indian independence struggle were imprisoned in Kalapani. The Cellular Jail is located in the Andaman Islands in the Bay of Bengal, 1,255 and 1,151 km from Kolkata and Madras respectively. The Andaman Islands have been used as a prison camp by the British since the Sepoy Mutiny of 1857. However, no separate prison was built at that time. On 12 June 189, it was decided to establish this colony in the Andaman Islands of India. Finally, in 1793, as part of that colony, cellular prisons were built. In just three years, in 1896, the construction work of Kalapani was completed by the tireless work of about six hundred prisoners day and night. It is like digging one's own grave with one's own hands and arranging for others to sleep in that grave. In the first anti-British movement, the rebels did not get along well with the British. Most of the rebels were suppressed by assassination, and the rest were sent into exile in the Andamans with life imprisonment. Hundreds of rebels who took part in the Sepoy Mutiny were sent to the Andamans under the supervision of prison guard David Barry and military physician Major James Pattison Walker.

The number of prisoners is slowly increasing, and the resentment of the prisoners is much higher than this number. Clearing the forest, cutting wood, fetching water - while doing these things, they see innumerable corpses here and there. Meanwhile, some British visitors came and declared the place unsuitable for human habitation. But the British authorities did not listen to those words. Where else could there be a safer place to hide political prisoners? Prison authorities released the prisoner as soon as he told them that he had escaped and died. Meanwhile, on April 18, 238 prisoners escaped from the jail and were caught. 6 of them were hanged. There is nothing different about the rest. Those who did not have the good fortune to die at once, the barbaric British without their world. Unable to bear the inhuman torture, some would go insane, some would die prematurely. In this way, they are making a mockery in the name of justice by arresting the protesting people who are raising their voices against the colonial rule day by day. Most of the prisoners were arrested from Bengal and Burma. Prisoners were terrified of the strong currents and the black water of the Andamans, and it was almost impossible to cross this path by swimming. There is no way out of this desolate island. Therefore, Kalapani became a favorite place of the British to punish the freedom fighters. They were chained and forced to build new homes on the island, including prisons, where British exploiters spent their days in comfort. Prisoners were also forced to build jetties in the Andamans to further strengthen colonialism. In the late nineteenth century, when India's independence was taking the form of a coup d'tat, the need for high-security prisons for arrested political prisoners became vital. Sir Charles James, the

Home Secretary of the British Raj, and Surgeon General of the British Administration. S. Lathbridge suggested that the Andaman Cellular Jail should provide harsher punishments for inmates who have been deported, with a minimum term. If everyone died like this in the field, it would be more noticeable to the people of India. With that in mind, Kalapani was created in the Andamans by combining innumerable tiny cells.

# Half-naked fakir

Mahatma Gandhi started a lawlessness movement by breaking the 'Salt Act' after the historic Dandi campaign. Across India, on the one hand, the Satyagraha movement has gained momentum, on the other hand, revolutionaries who believe in armed struggle like Bhagat Singh, Chandrasekhar Azad, Asfaqullah Khan, Surya Sen have also become active. Communist leaders like Muzaffar Ahmed, Saukat Usmani, PC Joshi, Radharman Mitra have been arrested in the Meerut conspiracy case in an attempt to overthrow the British rule. All in all, a turbulent political situation in India. The British government understood that it would not get wet easily. At least an agreement is needed with the Congress. The first round table meeting has already failed without the presence of the Congress, they cannot be ignored in determining the fate of India. Congress means Mohandas Karamchand Gandhi. The local and foreign political astrologers who had predicted non-violent non-cooperation and after the Chaurichaura incident, Gandhi had no more public support or mass base, started scratching their heads at the sight of the mass flood. The satyagrahis did not back down from indiscriminately charging sticks with Gandhi's name in Dharsana salt shell. In his name, Khan Abdul Ghaffar Khan's Lalkorta forces in the North-West Frontier

Province let him get a book in front of a police rifle. Gradually, Prime Minister Ramsay MacDonald and Viceroy Irwin realized that there was no way out of the stalemate without Gandhiji. The Viceroy summoned him to Delhi to discuss autonomy. The right-wing Conservatives, led by Churchill, were furious. They took the Labor-Liberal government by storm - what is the point of negotiating with them again? Traitors, not a word with the opposition. The whip needs to be straightened. Winston Churchill's immortal quote in this context - "It is alarming and also nauseating to see Mr. Gandhi, an Inner Temple lawyer, now become a seditious fakir of a type well known in the East, striding half-naked up the steps of the Viceregal Palace , while he is still organizing and conducting a defiant campaign of civil disobedience, to parley on equal terms with the representative of the King-Emperor. " He said that Gandhi should be tied up and thrown on the streets of Delhi and the viceroy's elephant should be carried over him. Irwin, however, did nothing of the sort. He was responsible for the interests of the British Empire, but personally liked Gandhi. When asked about Gandhi's clothes, he replied, 'Even our Lord Jesus Christ did not wear too much clothes. Mr. Gandhi did nothing reprehensible. ' After hearing about Gandhi's dress like Churchill, the viceroy added, "Many people were upset to see the Lord Jesus." It is Churchill's statement that gives rise to the word 'half-naked fakir'. Churchill and the Tories continued to use this term to describe Gandhi. Note that during the second round table meeting, when Gandhiji went to meet the king wearing the same khaddar, questions were raised about his sense of grandeur. The news media asked him if he was wearing clothes suitable for the situation according to his own opinion? Gandhiji also replied in a perfect manner - 'The King had on enough for both of us. ' There is a small conclusion to this story. About a decade later. In 1944, Churchill became Prime Minister. His anger at Gandhi did not abate. His first question was 'Is Gandhi dead?' Meanwhile, the unimaginable reality of partition is emerging from the womb of the future. There is still some hope that it can be avoided, but Gandhi knows that his followers like Sardar Vallabhbhai Patel, Chakravarti Rajagopalachari, Rajendra Prasad, Jawaharlal Nehru, Maulana Azad have also accepted partition with a real mind and are willing to share power with Jinnah. It is more desirable for them to divide the country as it is for Jinnah. He did not accept this reality as long as he was alive. He was the only one to die, except for a handful of followers like Acharya Kripalini and Khan Abdul Ghaffar Khan. Power is almost at hand, the need of the father of the nation is over. However, he took the pen to write a letter to the Prime Minister of the United Kingdom saying that he would try his best. Dear Prime Minister, You are reported to have a desire to crush the simple 'Naked Fakir' as you are said to have described me. I have been long trying to be a 'Fakir' and that naked - a more difficult task. I, therefore, regard the expression as a compliment though unintended. I approach you then as such and ask you to trust and use me for the sake of your people and mine and through them those of the world. Your sincere friend, M. K. Gandhi Churchill received the letter, but it was too late. And he did not answer. Because he knew that the biggest goal of his hated 'half-naked fakir' life, a united independent India, was about to fail. And that failure is coming at the hands of the followers of Fakir who jump into the greed for power. There is no need to discuss Gandhi directly, as he wants in this letter. He is empty, his followers abandoned, tired and frustrated. History does not write anything, but it is conceivable that the Prime Minister smiled with this letter in his hand. Whether the half-naked fakir has really lost everything so far.

# History of the Victoria Memorial Hall

The Victoria Memorial Hall was built to commemorate Queen Victoria of England at the famous Average Ground in Kolkata. The Queen died in 1901 at the age of 94. Lovely portrait of Queen Victoria of England. In his memory, the Victoria Memorial Hall was founded on 4 January 1906 by the then Prince of Wales and later by King George V. Construction of the building was completed on December 28, 1921. The building was inaugurated by the then Prince of Wales and later King Edward VIII. The Victoria Memorial Hall is one of the greatest architectures of British India. It is a combination of artwork from multiple countries. It is made of Italian style statues, Mughal style domes and marble like the Taj Mahal. This is the first and best example of European architecture in India. Established on a total of 64 acres of dummy. It was designed by Sir William Emerson. It was supervised by Vincent Esch, the then Eastern Railway Assistant Engineer. He gained considerable reputation in construction at that time. The theme of the design was a monument in the garden as well as a museum rich in relics commemorating British rule. Martin & Company was commissioned to build this famous monument. The total cost of construction of this building is estimated at Rs. 1,05,00,000. The marble stone of the building to build it weighed 80,000 tons. This stone was brought from Makrana in Rajasthan. The money that has been spent is collected entirely from businessmen and native states and voluntarily. The building is 103.32 meters long and 69.49 meters wide. The height of the statue 'Angel of Victory' is 56.08 meters. The main entrance to the Victoria Memorial Hall is the gateway. Winter is usually October to February, the best time to visit Victoria Memorial. The gate closes at 10:00 a.m. to 5:00 p.m. (Closed every Monday.) Also, special holidays: 26th January, 25th December, 2nd October, Eid-ul-Fitr, etc. Entrance fee: 10 rupees per head and 150 rupees per foreigner. 4 rupees per head to enter the garden. Usually such a beautiful arrangement for children. Admission to the museum is different. You have to buy a separate ticket. (Check the current rate charge before entering.) Victoria Memorial Hall. It is now maintained by the Indian Ministry of Culture. Sound and light is opposite the main gate. It runs daily from 6:00 pm to 8:30 pm. Take a look if you can. It costs 10 rupees to enter. Very enjoyable. Now the question is, why did it take so long to build this famous monument. The main reason, though, is that Lord Curzon oversees the work, the reluctance of subsequent rulers. There are 25 galleries here. There are statues of famous personalities of the English. Notable among them are portraits of McLean, Kipling, Windsor, Bishop Herrer, Eliam Hickey, Lord Clive, Warren Hastings, Lord Cornwallis, Lord Wellesley, Lord Dalhousie and others. Moreover, there are some statues of the wise men of that time. Among them are portraits of Keshab Chandra Sen, Michael Madhusudan Dutt, Rabindranath Tagore, Prince Dwarkanath Tagore and others.

www.ingramcontent.com/pod-product-compliance
Lightning Source LLC
LaVergne TN
LVHW100338181026
850499LV00039B/1133
*9789356102101*